**Still in My Heart**

Copyright © 2025 *Cassie Porter*

All Rights Reserved.

This book is subject to the condition that no part of this book is to be reproduced, transmitted in any form or means; electronic or mechanical, stored in a retrieval system, photocopied, recorded, scanned, or otherwise. Any of these actions require the proper written permission of the author.

All personal names in the following narrative are fictitious.

To Jen,

This collection is for you, the muse of every word, every melody, and every quiet thought that has filled my days and nights. It is a reflection of the love that shaped us, the heartbreak that tested us, and the unwavering hope that true love endures beyond it all. You will always be the song my heart sings and the light my soul remembers.

These pages are my way of saying what my heart has always known: I will always love you.

Though our paths may have diverged, I remain here, waiting for the day you find your way back-- to yourself, to us, to the love that was and can still be. May these pages remind you of the person who will always hold you close and has never stopped loving you. Until then, know that you are forever in my heart, the song my soul will always sing.

# Contents

Where Scars Turn to Strength ............................................... 5
Whispered to the Stars ........................................................... 7
Where Love Belongs ............................................................... 9
Chasing Shadows ................................................................... 11
Steady and True ..................................................................... 13
The Weight of Waiting .......................................................... 15
The Cost of Loving You ........................................................ 17
Stuck in the Verse .................................................................. 20
Chasing What Won't Stay ..................................................... 23
Waiting for Your Heart ......................................................... 26
Too Deep to Hold You ........................................................... 29
Shadows of Heartbreak ......................................................... 31
The Weight of Friendship ..................................................... 33
To Jen, My Heart's Hollow ................................................... 35
Where Love Grows Without End ......................................... 38
Erased in a Moment .............................................................. 41
When Actions Speak Louder Than Words ......................... 44
Where Are You, My Friend .................................................. 47
When You Realize .................................................................. 49
When Friendship Fades Away .............................................. 51
Without You ........................................................................... 53

## Where Scars Turn to Strength

I see the shadows you've carried inside,
The quiet battles you never let slide.
We both wore armor, both bore scars,
Chasing dreams beneath distant stars.

I know I fell short, let you down,
Lost myself, wore a heavy crown.
But I've woken now, my heart beats clear,
Ready to love, to fight, to steer.

I see the laughter we once would share,
The wild, untamed, fearless pair.
Dancing through life with an open hand,
Chasing horizons, daring to stand.

Trust me, love, I've got you now,
I'll learn each piece; I'll show you how.
Together, we'll heal, we'll mend, we'll grow,
Reclaim the fire we used to know.

A life of passion, a love that roars,
Adventure waiting behind new doors.
Through valleys and peaks, both storm and sun,
I'll hold your heart until we're one.

So take my hand, let's start anew,
A journey meant for just us two.
I love you fiercely, I love you whole,
You are my heart, my home, my soul.

## Whispered to the Stars

I had to say goodbye, let her go,
though my heart screams, aching to know
why she'd choose another over this ---
the love we built, the warmth, the kiss.

I hold my ground, though I fall apart,
clinging to pieces of my shattered heart.
She chose to walk, to close the door,
leaving memories scattered across the floor.

But universe hear my silent plea,
bring her back, set her spirit free.
Guide her steps, let her see anew
the life we dreamed, that love so true.

I'll wait in the shadows, standing still,
holding space for the heart I fill.
Let her find her way ---
bring her home, let her choose to stay.

## Where Love Belongs

I had to let her go tonight,
though everything in me held tight---
she chose another, a path away,
leaving the life we built to fray.

But the universe, hear what I know inside:
she's mine, my love, my light, my guide.
Bring her back, let her heart turn,
to the home we made, for which I yearn.

Through every shadow, I'll remain
steadfast in love, through joy and pain.
For she's the one I'm meant to hold,
a truth as certain as the stars, as bold.

Let her see where she's meant to be,
right here, in our love's eternity.

## Chasing Shadows

You hold my past like a weapon in hand,
A mirror reflecting who I used to stand.
But can't you see how I've broken the chains?
How I've risen from the ashes and embraced the change?

I've fought through the storms, rebuilt from the wreck,
Placed my heart on my sleeve, no mask to protect.
Yet your eyes look through me as if I'm not here,
Chasing a ghost that will always disappear.

You reach for the echoes, the whispers, the haze,
Ignoring the light I've been burning for days.
I've grown, I've mended, I've learned how to give,
But you turn from the love that still wants to live.

I am not the shadow you're running behind,
I am flesh, I am heart, I am present in time.
Yet you'd rather pursue what can never be real
Than embrace the love that I'm here to reveal.

I'll stand in this truth, though it cuts me apart
Because my love is whole; it beats from my heart.
But I can't make you see what you choose to deny,
So I'll let you chase shadows while I learn to fly.

## Steady and True

I wasn't in a good place that much is true,
And our love bore the weight of what I didn't pursue.
Our story was strong, a bond deep and rare,
But I let it falter when I wasn't there.

I've changed for myself, for us, for the light,
It didn't take ten years to know what was right.
It didn't take decades to show what you mean,
To hold up a mirror to the love I've seen.

Yet you chase the familiar, though it brought you pain,
A path with footprints of heartbreak and disdain.
Someone who hurt you, crosses lines without care,
Who takes and consumes but is never quite there.

I stand here, not pleading, but steady and true,
A version of me who has grown through and through.
Not perfect, not finished, but worthy of love,
Of kindness, of trust, of the stars above.

I hope one day you see the choices you make,
The pieces you give and the ones that she takes.
And if that day comes, know I was always near,
Not waiting, but hoping you'll see clear.

## The Weight of Waiting

Seven years, we wove our thread,
A life together, a love unsaid.
But now I wonder, was it real?
Or just a place to stand still, to heal?

If she was the one who held your heart,
Why let me play the lover's part?
Did you see me, or just the space I filled,
A silent witness to a dream unfulfilled?

Why wait for her to come back through,
To tear apart what I thought was true?
Was I the pause in a story, not mine,
A fleeting moment, lost in time?

Who was I in your tangled plan?
A lifeboat, a shadow, a stand-in man?
Was my love enough to make you stay,
Or just a shelter until that day?

I gave you all I had to give,
A reason to hope, a life to live.
But now it feels like I was blind,
Loving someone who was biding time.

Tell me, Jen, was it ever real?
Did you ever love or only feel
The weight of waiting, the pull of her,
While I was drowning, unsure?

I need to know, though it breaks my soul,
Were you whole with me, or half of a whole?
Did you stay for me, or just to get by,
Until her name lit up your sky?

## The Cost of Loving You

I was the one who held you near,
When shadows whispered doubt and fear.
You let me in, or so it seemed,
While chasing echoes of a dream.

Was I the pause in your restless chase,
 A fleeting comfort, a borrowed space?
While I gave you my heart, steady and true,
You waited for her to come back to you.

And when she did, with scars still fresh,
You cast me aside like yesterday's flesh. F
or the one who broke you, time and again,
You traded the love of a loyal friend.

Yet here I stand, despite the ache,
Carrying pain for your heart's sake.
Though I feel the sting of being used,
I'd endure it all just to see you refuse.

Refuse the hurt and the lies you've been fed,
The broken paths that lead nowhere instead.
For true love isn't meant to keep score,
It gives, even when it can take no more.

Each day, I relive the hollowed-out sting,
The weight of the loss, the ache it brings.
But you're worth the wound, the endless strife,
Because loving you feels larger than life.

So, I'll show you love in its purest form,
Even as my heart weathers the storm.
And though you've thrown me to the side,
I'll love you still through all my pride.

For love doesn't fade, even when bruised,
Even when shattered, even when used.
I'll bear this burden, I'll bear the cost,
Because loving you is worth being lost.

## Stuck in the Verse

You were a melody, a song from the past,
Echoes of laughter, but the shadows were cast.
Ten years later, the rhythms still play,
But you're stuck in the same tune, drifting away.

I watched you run in circles, chasing your own tail,
While we could've built a future, you chose to derail.

You're lost in the echoes of who you used to be,
Repeating old patterns, while you're losing me.
Your heart's still singing those familiar lines,
But I'm here waiting, hoping for new signs.

We had a chance to write a brand-new song,
But you cling to the past, where you think you belong.
Every note a reminder of the love we could share,
But you're dancing alone, and I'm left in despair.

Thought we could change the story, turn the page tonight,
But you keep rewriting it, lost in the night.

You're lost in the echoes of who you used to be,
Repeating old patterns, while you're losing me.
Your hearts still singing those familiar lines,
But I'm here waiting, hoping for new signs.

You say you want more, but you settle for her,
Clinging to the past and the pain that occurred.
You're stuck in old feelings of what you once knew,
While I'm here with my heart aching for you.
You keep playing the same, tired song.

You're lost in the echoes of who you used to be,
Repeating old patterns, while you're losing me.
Your hearts still singing those familiar lines,
But I'm here waiting, hoping for new signs.

So I'll keep on dreaming while you find your way.

But I won't be a ghost, just a shadow to sway.

If you ever wake up to see where true love lies,

Know my heart will be waiting; no more compromise.

# Chasing What Won't Stay

You say you're following the call of your heart,
But it's leading you back to where you fell apart.
You're chasing a ghost who left you behind,
Trading real love for a figment of time.

I gave you my all, I stayed through the storms,
Built us a home where your soul felt warm.
But now you're running to an empty flame,
To someone who'd never do the same.

This is your choice to leave, your chance to fall,
You're giving up on the best of it all.
I'd never let go, I'd see it through,
But you're choosing the selfish over someone who loves you.

You think it's your heart, but it's fear you obey,
Running back to a love that threw you away.
I put you first in every single way,
But you're trading that for someone who takes.

I was the light when your nights were dark,
The steady beat of your fragile heart.
But now you're choosing the path you know,
Even if it leads where nothing will grow.

This is your choice to leave, your chance to fall,
You're giving up on the best of it all.
I'd never let go, I'd see it through,
But you're choosing the selfish over someone who loves you.

I hope you see it when the glow fades out,
When the love you're chasing fills you with doubt.
I hope you remember what you had with me,
And the cost of trading truth for fantasy.

This is your chance to leave, your chance to fall,
You're giving up on the best of it all.
I'm still here, strong, unshaken, and true,
But you're choosing the selfish over someone who loves you.

You're walking away from a heart that won't break,

For a dream that's a lie, a mistake you'll remake.

You think it's your heart, but it's just old scars

Leading you back to a life below the stars.

I put you first; you were my guiding star,

But you're chasing a shadow that won't catch your heart.

# Waiting for Your Heart

You said goodbye, and it cut through my heart,
(She said goodbye, she tore you apart.)
She pulled you back, and I lost you to the past,
(But love like ours, it was built to last.)

Oh, I'm waiting, waiting, waiting for your heart,
(I'm waiting, I'm waiting, never wanted to part.)
Yeah, I'm waiting, waiting, waiting for your heart,
(Love grows slow; it's a beautiful art.)

Time goes by as the river flows wide,
(But in my dreams, you're always by my side.)
Friendships blend in the colors of pain,
(We rise again, always stronger from the rain.)

Oh, I'm waiting, waiting, waiting for your heart,
(I'm waiting, I'm waiting, never wanted to part.)
Yeah, I'm waiting, waiting, waiting for your heart,
(Love grows slow; it's a beautiful art.)

Through the shadows, I'll take each step,
(With every heartbeat, our dreams are kept.)
We've grown together through laughter and tears,
(Let's face tomorrow, no more fears.)

Oh, I'm waiting, waiting, waiting for your heart,
(I'm waiting, I'm waiting, never wanted to part.)
Yeah, I'm waiting, waiting, waiting for your heart,
(Love grows slow; it's a beautiful art.)

So here I stand, with hope in my hands,
(Our love's a garden, let's nurture the plans.)
If you find your way back to where we start,
(You'll see forever, waiting in my heart.)

Oh, I'm waiting, waiting, waiting for your heart,
(I'm waiting, I'm waiting, never wanted to part.)
Yeah, I'm waiting, waiting, waiting for your heart,
(Love grows slow; it's a beautiful art.)

Waiting for your heart, waiting for your heart,

(I'm waiting, I'm waiting, come back, don't depart.)

Waiting for your heart, waiting for your heart,

(Love will find a way; we'll never be apart.)

Waiting for your heart...

(Waiting for your heart...)

(Oh, I'm waiting...)

(For your heart...)

## Too Deep to Hold You

My love for you runs fierce and deep,
a river vast, a tide too steep.
It's boundless, wild---a flame, a storm,
a love too fierce to keep you warm.

I tried to hold it, tried to stay,
but love like this can't find a way
to keep you close, to let you breathe---
you need the space that I can't leave.

So go, my love, you have to be
far from the weight of loving me.
I love you far too much to stay;
to truly keep you, I must let you go.

Know that my heart will always burn,
a quiet flame until you return.
But loving you means letting go,
for my love's too deep, and you must know.

## Shadows of Heartbreak

In shadows where our laughter lay,
A whispered promise slipped away.
You sought comfort in a past so cruel,
A haunting ghost that played the fool.

I gave you all, my heart, my time,
But love turned bitter, turned to grime.
You turned to her, a fleeting spark,
And left me tangled in the dark.

Numbness wraps me like a shroud,
A heavy fog, a silent crowd.
Days stretch on, an endless night.
I search for stars that lost their light.

I hate her for the love she stole,
For weaving pain into my soul.
Yet deep inside, I hate you too,
For choosing shadows over what is true.

But still, I'll wait, through every tear,

For brighter days to draw you near.

A fragile hope, though hearts may break,

Will guide me through this aching ache.

For now, I grieve, but I won't fall,

In time, I'll rise above it all.

Though love has left a jagged scar,

I'll mend my wings; I'll reach for stars.

## The Weight of Friendship

Thank you for showing up that day,
When life had stripped my strength away.
You were the friend I needed most,
A steady hand, a guiding post.

But you still hold on to who I was,
An anxious heart, a soul on pause.
I know it weighed on us before,
Yet that's not me---not anymore.

I've found my fire, my fearless spark,
A brighter path, no longer dark.
I crave the world, the city's glow,
Adventures only we would know.

But when I asked for just one thing,
You couldn't come without the wall.
Her presence there, a price to pay,
A sacrifice I had to face.

Still, I bent, though my heart did ache,
For you, it's a choice I'd always make.
Each heavy cost, I'd gladly bear,
Because you're worth it, beyond compare.

If only you could see me now---
The weightless truth, the unmade vow.
To roam, to dream, to simply be,
I wish you'd see the real me.

Thank you, my friend,
for all you've shown,
For lifting me when I was alone.
And though life's path may twist and bend,
I'll always, always call you friend.

## To Jen, My Heart's Hollow

Jen, I miss you more than words can say,

The silence echoes where your laughter used to play.

You weren't just love, you became my home,

Now I'm here, lost, with no place to roam.

It sucks to feel this emptiness inside,

To long for the warmth where you used to reside.

Family isn't just a name, a title, or a place—

It's the feeling of knowing you're safe and embraced.

But now, there's space where you should be,

A vacant room, a gap in me.

There's no one to call when the night is cold,

No hand to hold when I start to fold.

I thought we'd always be together, no end in sight,

But now I'm left in shadows, longing for light.

You weren't just my partner; you were my everything,

The one who made me feel like I had roots like I had wings.

Now those wings are clipped, and I fall alone,

Grieving for the love that's now unknown.

I've got no one else; you were my only,

The one who knew me, truly and wholly.

And though I'm trying to understand,

It's hard to stand with no hand in hand.

So I'm left with the ache, the unanswered calls,

Wondering if you miss me at all.

This distance cuts deeper than any sword,

I'm grieving for the family I can't afford.

Jen, if you're listening, hear my plea—

I need you like air, like the roots of a tree.

I miss you so much; it hurts to breathe,

But I still believe in us and what we could be.

# Where Love Grows Without End

Jen, my love, where do I start?
With all the pieces of my heart?
I see the weight that you still bear,
The quiet doubts, the whispered care.

Your fears like shadows in the night,
A battle fought with fading light.
But, love, I know the strength you hold,
A fire that's burning, yet untold.

Within this home, with every touch,
I see the things we long for much:
A place to rest, a place to grow,
Where love can bloom and gently flow.

I know you seek peace, a way,
To quiet all the noise and fray.
Your heart, so tender,
needs to find the quiet place, the peace of mind.

But love, my love, if you will see,
In every moment, you're with me.
This house, this life we've yet to make,
Is built on trust, with no mistake.

I'll be the steady in your storm,
The warmth to keep your heart so warm.
No end in sight, no fading part,
A home that grows with every start.

So take your time, and know it true,
This love I offer all for you.
Within these walls, we'll both be free—
Together, love, just you and me.

We'll find the peace we both deserve,
Where joy and laughter gently curve,
And in this space, with hearts entwined,
No end, no fear, just love defined.

# Erased in a Moment

You didn't need space, you didn't ask for time,
You just walked away without reason, no rhyme.
Seven years, built on trust and care,
Gone in an instant, without a prayer.

I heard the words, "I cheated," and still,
I didn't leave—I stayed, I would heal.
I didn't walk out, didn't run from the fight,
I changed, Jen; I changed overnight.

You didn't ask, you didn't plead,
But I saw the pain, so I took the lead.
I changed who I was, made things right,
I fought for us with all of my might.

But you, you walked without looking back
While I was rebuilding what you seemed to lack.
I stood by your side through your darkest days,
But you turned your back, went your own ways.

I didn't run, I didn't hide,
I gave you my heart, I stood by your side.
You chose a feeling—fleeting and new,
While I stayed true, but it wasn't enough for you.

Seven years down the drain in a blink,
You traded it all for a feeling, a blink.
I gave you my love, I gave you my soul,
But you threw it all away and lost control.

How do you just forget what we had?
How do you erase what was good and bad?
I didn't walk away, I didn't just leave,
I stayed, I loved, I tried to believe.

But you, Jen, you didn't wait,
You chose someone else to fill your state.
A feeling, a rush, over what was real,
And now I'm left with nothing but steel.

You say you want to be friends, like before,
But how do you heal what you've ignored?
Seven years of love and devotion,
Thrown away like it was just a mere notion.

I gave you my heart, I gave you my best,
I was ready to prove it, to pass the test.
But now you're gone, and I'm left with the cost,
Seven years gone, and I'm left feeling lost.

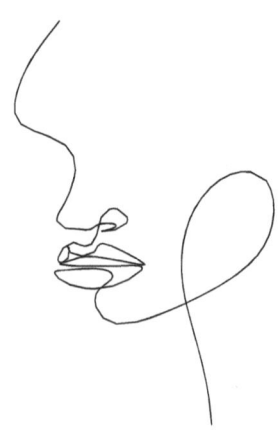

# When Actions Speak Louder Than Words

You say you haven't changed, that you're still the same,

But the Jen I loved would never play this game.

She wouldn't vanish when things got tough,

Wouldn't turn away when the going got rough.

When life felt heavy, when I needed a friend,

You'd be there, without question, again and again.

But now, when I'm struggling, when I'm feeling alone,

You've pushed me aside, left me on my own.

I know it's okay to chase the life you desire,

But it's not okay to leave me in the fire.

You can go after what you think you need,

But you don't have to treat me like I'm a weed.

You've replaced me so easily like I was never there,

Like our bond meant nothing like you didn't care.

You were never a liar, never a cheat,

But now, your actions don't align with what you preach.

The Jen I knew wouldn't toss love aside,

Wouldn't throw away a friend and then hide.

But now, with her here, it's clear you've changed,

Your heart, your loyalty, feels so estranged.

It's okay to grow, to chase something new,

But it's not okay to act like I never mattered to you.

You say you haven't changed, but your actions speak loud,

And they're telling me you've lost what made you proud.

I stood by you, gave you my trust,

But now it's like you've erased it all, turned it to dust.

So go after the life you think you need,

But don't forget the one who helped you grow and still believes.

You can move on, but you can't erase

The love and the friendship you discarded in haste.

I'll always remember the Jen I once knew,

But I can't forget how quickly she gave up on someone loyal and true.

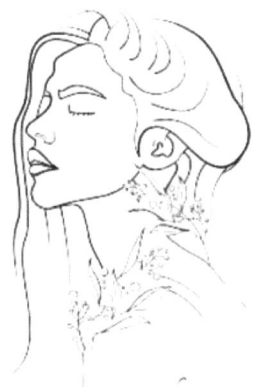

# Where Are You, My Friend

I've stood by you through all the fight,
When days were dark and felt no light.
I've given all and asked for none,
A friend to lean on when all was undone.

But when I needed you when I was torn,
You couldn't show up, though I was worn.
You needed her there for you to stay,
And I had to give in to make it okay.

I brought her in, though it tore me apart,
Hoping you'd show up, just with your heart.
But why can't you be there without the price?
Why does my pain feel like a sacrifice?

I've given so much just to stay strong,
But it feels like I'm the one in the wrong.
When will I be enough, as I stand,
Without needing her to complete your plan?

I've given my all, but where's your return?
When will you show up without me having to burn?
Will I always need to give, to make you see,
Of will you ever stand for me, like a friend should be?

## When You Realize

Jen, you say you don't want me,
But I didn't wait—I've changed, I've grown,
For myself, for you, for us,
Yet still, it's not enough to keep you whole.

You're searching for a feeling,
Something that's fleeting, something new,
But love like ours can grow beyond
The fire that fades, the spark you knew.

I've given all, but it's not enough,
You want more than what we've built,
But what you seek is just a shadow,
A moment that time will melt.

When you find that nothing out there
Will match the depth of what we've shared,
I'll be here, waiting,
With love that's patient, deep, and rare.

So, take your time, go chase your dream,
But know this truth when you're alone—
Our love was never just a feeling—
It's a life, a home, a place to grow.

# When Friendship Fades Away

Seven years we built, through thick and thin,
A friendship, a love, a world within.
You were my family, my safe, steady place,
The only warmth in life's cold embrace.

But now the holidays come, hollow and bare,
And I sit here alone while you're elsewhere.
You knew my heart, the emptiness I face,
Yet you've left me stranded, no trace, no grace.

Do you remember the promises we'd keep,
The laughter that carried us when life cut deep?
Now, the silence is louder than the words we said,
And I wonder if you mourn what we've left for dead.

I have no family to lean upon,
No arms to hold me when all feels gone.
You knew this truth; it wasn't concealed,
Yet you've let me wounded, the pain revealed.

The holidays ache where they once brought light;
a season of joy now feels like night.
Not just the loss of the love we knew,
But the absence of the friend I had in you.

I don't ask for pity or a change of heart,
Just to know that you cared as we drifted apart.
Seven years is not something you throw away,
And yet I'm alone on this holiday.

## Without You

You are the pulse within my chest,
The quiet rhythm that grants me rest.
Without you, there's no light in the sky,
No reason to laugh; no need to try.

You are the air that fills my lungs,
The whispered calm when the world is spun.
In every breath, in every sigh,
You're the reason the days go by.

Our home, without you, is a hollow shell,
A place where echoes of silence dwell.
But when you're here, it's warmth and grace,
A haven where time slows its chase.

You bring the calm when storms arise,
The peace that shines behind your eyes.
Without you, love, I can't pretend—
There's no beginning, no middle, no end.

I can't exist without your heart,
Without you, I'd fall apart.
You are the life I hold so tight,
My morning sun, my star at night.

So here I stand, with love so true—
This world, this life, is nothing without you.

www.ingramcontent.com/pod-product-compliance
Lightning Source LLC
Chambersburg PA
CBHW041216070526
44583CB00001B/10